INCREDIBLY DISGUSTING FOOD™

SALTY AND SUGARY SNACKS

THE INCREDIBLY DISGUSTING STORY

Adam Furgang

New York

To Caleb, who loves to snack on grapes and strawberries

Published in 2011 by The Rosen Publishing Group, Inc.
29 East 21st Street, New York, NY 10010

First Edition

Library of Congress Cataloging-in-Publication Data

Furgang, Adam.
Salty and sugary snacks: the incredibly disgusting story / Adam Furgang.
    p. cm.—(Incredibly disgusting food)
Includes bibliographical references and index.
ISBN 978-1-4488-1267-7 (library binding)
ISBN 978-1-4488-2283-6 (pbk.)
ISBN 978-1-4488-2287-4 (6-pack)
1. Snack foods—Health aspects—Juvenile literature. 2. Salt—Health aspects—Juvenile literature. 3. Sugar—Health aspects—Juvenile literature. I. Title.
TP451.S57F87 2011
613.2—dc22

2010025751

Manufactured in the United States of America

CPSIA Compliance Information: Batch #W11YA: For further information, contact Rosen Publishing, New York, New York, at 1-800-237-9932.

CONTENTS

INTRODUCTION

The three traditional meals of the day—breakfast, lunch, and dinner—now have a new partner: the sugary and salty snack. North Americans' favorite junk foods are easier to find than ever before, and the snack industry is growing by leaps and bounds. Snack food makers take in more than $65 billion annually.

The availability of more snacks—and a wider variety of snacks—may sound like good news. However, North Americans' increased intake of snack foods has extremely negative consequences on their health. Increases in many serious diseases are on the rise, and many of them are being seen in younger and younger people. Much of the blame for this alarming trend is placed on excessive consumption of processed sugary and salty snacks.

North Americans are consuming these snacks in greater and greater quantities. Between the mid-1970s and the mid-1990s, for example, U.S. consumption of salty snack foods more than doubled. Consumption of sugary snacks rose a great deal during this period as well. Unfortunately, children are the main consumers of these disease-promoting snack foods.

While both sugar and salt are natural food substances and salt is something the human body requires, they are healthy only in limited quantities and not very frequently. Throughout human history, foods did not contain a lot of naturally occurring sugar or salt. People had to eat fresh seasonal fruits at just the right time to get natural sugar and a rare sweet treat. Today, sugary treats are far too easy to come by. In fact, they are extremely difficult to ignore or avoid.

The phrase "you are what you eat" is more true than most of us realize. What we put into our bodies can either help or hinder our weight control, energy levels, mood, health, and lifestyle. Being aware of what we are eating is the first step in eating fewer of these incredibly disgusting foods.

1

TOO MUCH OF A TASTY THING?

The idea of eating spoonfuls of pure salt or sugar may be disgusting to imagine. Yet when people continue to eat unhealthy snacks between and after every meal, they are putting huge and dangerous amounts of sugar and salt into their bodies. And it is destroying their health. Today, many processed snacks include far too much sugar and salt. There is nothing mysterious or secretive about their presence in snack foods. They are hiding in plain sight, listed right on the ingredient labels. Even many snack foods that are considered "healthy," such as breakfast bars, energy bars, canned soup, and whole wheat breads, contain surprising amounts of salt and sugar.

In order to function properly, the body needs a large variety of nutrients from many sources. Natural sugar and salt are two such nutrients. So it is normal for humans to crave them to some degree. But the foods in our grocery stores make these ingredients far too easy to come by, so we tend to get much more than the small amounts that our bodies actually require.

Incredibly Disgusting Mass Production

Today, snacks are manufactured on a huge scale and delivered all around the globe. The world's ever-growing love for tasty snacks has led to an increase in food production and has caused the manufacturing industry to work more efficiently. As with any business, snack companies are constantly trying to decrease production costs, so they have come up with ways to save money. One way is to produce more goods at once. Another way is to create new ingredients that make manufacturing the food less expensive and provide the product with a longer shelf life. As a result, snack foods are now more commonplace, plentiful, and highly processed than ever before. None of this is good news from a health perspective.

Some of the ingredients in snack foods are surprising, as are their amounts. One such ingredient is high fructose corn syrup. This artificial sweetener is processed from corn and has become so cheap to make—far cheaper than refining raw sugarcane— that it is now put into sugary

The snack food industry has made it easier than ever to just grab some salty and sugary snacks on the run.

snack foods in alarmingly high quantities. More and more studies have linked overconsumption of this now common ingredient to many health problems, including obesity and diabetes. To be a healthy and informed consumer, it helps to know what is going into the food one eats.

The Sour Story of Sugar

Pure sugar is an organic compound that has a very high calorie content. Our bodies convert these sugar-derived calories into energy. The calories not burned up in energy are then stored as fat. In the past, naturally sugar-rich foods such as berries and other fruits grew only in local environments once a year. Human bodies evolved to crave and savor these foods so that they were sure to obtain the essential nutrients when the food became available and to help store fat for the times when it was not. Pure table sugar comes from sugarcane, a plant that grows in warm climates like South America and the Caribbean. Other natural sugars also come from bee honey and maple tree sap.

Today, despite the worldwide prevalence of sugar sources and refined sugar, consumers might have a hard time finding old-fashioned sugar listed as an ingredient in snack foods. This doesn't mean, however, that snacks are becoming healthier and less sweetened. There are now about forty different kinds of sweeteners found in modern snack foods. They are disguised with fancy names such as high fructose corn syrup, barley malt, dextrose, modified corn starch, beet sugar, fructose, sucrose, brown rice syrup, malt, sorbitol, invert sugar, fruit juice concentrate, glactose, lactose, polydextrose, turbanido sugar, mannitol, xylitol, and maltodextrin.

There are about forty processed chemicals used in snack foods that try to imitate the sweetness of this refined sugar.

Most people do not even know what most of these words mean. They just consume their snacks without thinking about it. They may never realize that each of these terms represents a form of sugar that will add unnecessary calories and weight to their bodies. Studies have shown that human bodies metabolize fructose differently from other sweeteners. Too much fructose can affect the liver—the organ that removes toxins from the body, aids in digestion, stores energy in the form of glycogen (a carbohydrate that is the storage form of glucose), and synthesizes proteins. Excessive sugar intake can damage the liver in the same way that too much alcohol can damage it. This is called a "fatty liver." The trend toward increased obesity in the United States began not long after industry-grade high fructose corn syrup was first mass produced in the 1980s. It is now a common ingredient in thousands of snacks.

Even those people who think they are carefully watching their diet and restricting their sugar intake may be surprised by how much sugar they are ingesting every day. The U.S. Food and Drug Administration (FDA) recommends no more than 1.4 ounces (40 grams) a day of added sugars. Four grams of sugar is equal to one teaspoon of

sugar, so therefore 40 grams equals ten teaspoons of sugar. If that sounds like a lot, consider that one 20-ounce (0.6 liter) bottle of typical fruit punch can have the equivalent of 18 teaspoons of sugar! And most of the time it's not even pure sugar but rather disgusting artificial chemical sweetener created in a lab.

The shocking story does not end there. A single serving of a chocolate candy bar can have as many as 0.88 ounces (25 g) of sugar. Red licorice can have 1.5 ounces (43 g) of sugar per serving. Chocolate-covered pretzels can have 0.7 ounces (20 g) of sugar. Even some brands of yogurt with fruit on the bottom, which many people believe is a "healthy" snack, can have 0.9 ounces (26 g) of sugar per serving. This means that people are often getting all their daily recommended amount of sugar in only one or two snack foods, even if they are "healthy" snacks.

Consider how typical it is to consume a cookie or muffin between breakfast and lunch, have a snack bar between lunch and dinner, and then eat a candy bar at the movie theater at night. It is easy to see how many calories are being put into our bodies from sugar alone—and how far above the daily recommended intake this amount of sugar is. And this is just from snack foods! Items such as ketchup, barbeque sauce, tomato sauce, and bread usually have high amounts of added sugars as well.

Over-Salted

Salt is a mineral that is needed by the body in order to perform a variety of different functions. The mineral sodium is present in salt. Sodium plays a role in maintaining the balance of water and other liquids in the body and blood cells. Sodium also helps properly regulate muscle contractions, heart rhythm, and nerve impulses. The human body cannot manufacture sodium by itself, so humans crave foods that contain salt. This craving helps ensure that people will eat food that contains sodium and thereby guarantee that some of the body's basic functions will continue to work smoothly and properly. Throughout

evolutionary history, the human tongue has developed very sensitive salt receptors. These receptors indicate to humans which foods contain sodium— an essential mineral needed for survival.

In modern times, however, processed snack foods have become overloaded with salt (or sodium, as it is commonly listed on ingredient labels). Salt is often added to improve the taste of many snacks. It is also used in many snack foods simply as a preservative to promote longer shelf life. Potato chips, corn and cheese puffs, corn chips, peanuts, pretzels, salsa, beef jerky, and crackers all have very high sodium content. Many common snack foods that one would not think are salty at all can contain sodium, too. Pudding, donuts, chocolate, ketchup, black licorice, and bagels all contain sodium, sometimes in far greater amounts than one might expect from a simple snack food.

Food labels must be read very carefully to see how much salt is actually hiding in snack foods.

Overweight vs. Obese

Being obese means that a person's body has an excessively high amount of body fat. It is possible to calculate how overweight a person is by determining his or her body mass index, also called a BMI. A mathematical formula measures a person's weight-to-height ratio. If you find you have a BMI of 25 to 29, you are considered to be overweight, and if you have a BMI of 30 or more, you are considered obese. Many good BMI calculators can be found online and can even suggest the ideal weight for your height and age.

The excessively high salt content in snack foods can have terrible effects on the body. Ingesting too much salt or sodium on a consistent basis upsets the body's natural balance of fluids and electrolytes. Electrolytes are substances that can conduct electricity. In this role, they help keep the body hydrated and regulate nerve and muscle function. An electrolyte and fluid imbalance can result in diseases and conditions such as hypertension (high blood pressure), osteoporosis (bone loss), stomach ulcers, heart disease, kidney stones, and kidney damage. Hypertension left unchecked can lead to heart attack and stroke.

The human body uses the sodium in salt that it needs and disposes of excess amounts in our waste. However, the body is not really designed to handle excess amounts of sodium. A person actually needs only about 0.01 ounces (200 milligrams) of sodium daily. The body cannot use more than this, and the excess must be removed from the body by the kidneys. The U.S. Food and Drug Administration recommends about 0.08 ounces (2,400 mg) daily. The American Heart Association recommends that sodium be limited to less than 0.05 ounces (1,500 mg) per day. Individuals with medical diagnosis such as kidney disease, congestive heart failure, hypertension, and diabetes may be required to further limit their sodium intake. On average, however, North Americans consume about 2 1/2 teaspoons a day or an alarmingly high 6,000 milligrams! That is more than twenty times what the body requires.

At this rate of consumption, the human body cannot get rid of the salt fast enough, so it builds up in the system. Fluid imbalances, water retention, and even weight gain all result from the buildup, and blood pressure spikes as well. A spike in blood pressure causes more strain on the veins and heart. The heart has to work harder to pump the blood at a higher pressure. Heart attack or stroke can eventually result from this excess blood pressure, as can severe kidney damage. Keep in mind, however, that salt is necessary, and not getting enough salt can cause low blood pressure, muscle cramps, dizziness, and electrolyte imbalance. Moderation in salt intake is essential.

Targeting Kids

Food companies have been marketing sweet and salty snack foods to children for decades now. While the occurrence of obesity and other illnesses related to sugary and salty snacks are still far too high, some changes are beginning to be made. According to a federal health and nutrition survey, about one-third of all U.S. children are overweight. Further, about 17 percent of American youth between the ages of two and nineteen are obese. This represents a huge increase in average weight among children over the past generation.

Vending machines filled with salty and sugary snacks—often located in schools—contribute to the obesity problem among North American children and teens.

In the past three decades, according to the Centers for Disease Control and Prevention (CDC), the national rate of obesity among Americans of all ages has more than doubled. This rate has more than tripled among teens during the same time period.

Many parents, students, and teachers alike are fed up with empty-calorie, high-carbohydrate, low-protein snack foods being sold to kids in vending machines. Often these vending machines are found right in the school cafeteria or hallways. As a result of these horrible diet trends, the Department of Education has issued new guidelines for what kinds of foods, snacks, and beverages can be sold and marketed to children. New guidelines would limit daily snack food calories to no more than 200, the sodium content to 0.01 ounces (200 mg), and added sugars to no more than 35 percent of the total snack calories. The message seems to be getting across. The percentage of American high schools and middle schools that sell sugary and salty snacks to their students in vending machines has recently dropped from 54 to 36 percent.

2

SHORT-TERM EFFECTS

Until relatively recently in human history, people did not sit down to eat three full meals every day. And they certainly weren't used to high-calorie snacking in between each meal. Even when food was readily available to people, it did not contain added and excessive amounts of sugar or salt. Berries and other fruits are some of the sweetest—and healthiest—foods in nature. Celery is an example of a natural and wholesome food that is high in salt, or sodium. Still, these foods are nowhere near as high in sugar or sodium as many of the industry-processed sugary and salty snacks North Americans eat today.

Humans crave salty foods because their bodies need sodium to regulate fluid balance and other essential systems. People need to eat food in order to generate the energy necessary to live and work. Eating more food than absolutely necessary even helped our ancestors to store up fat that their bodies could draw on for energy when food became scarce. However, the human body can store only so much extra fat before it begins to be negatively affected. When processed snacks are eaten in excess, the body's organs cannot work efficiently enough to process this abundance of sugars and salt, and overall health and well-being suffers as a result.

Sugar, Insulin, Glucose Regulation, and Weight Gain

When simple sugars are introduced into the body in huge quantities, and consistently over time, various organs become overwhelmed by the effort to process it all. The job of the pancreas is to produce a chemical hormone called insulin. Insulin is important because it regulates the amount of glucose in the blood. Glucose is a natural sugar that is produced during the digestion process and provides the body with energy. Insulin production goes into overdrive when a lot of sugar is consumed because glucose levels in the blood are rising and require regulation. Production of too much insulin keeps blood sugar levels high, converts more glucose to fat, and does not allow the body to burn some of its stored fat.

With no break between cookies, cakes, pies, and candy, day after day, there is no time for the breakdown of fat into energy to occur. The body keeps blindly producing insulin in an attempt to regulate the excessive levels of glucose in the blood. In the process, the insulin converts excess glucose into fat. Weight gain will result since the body is very good at converting sugar into fat. If the body becomes slightly overweight and poor eating

Children and teens who are obese are at risk of developing many serious, even life-threatening, diseases as they get older.

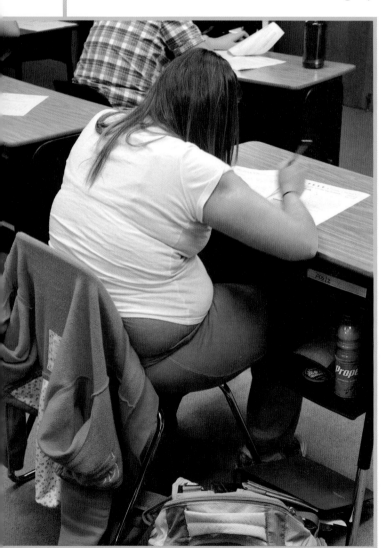

habits are not changed at this point, greater weight gain becomes very easy. A person can go from slightly overweight to very overweight to obese in a fairly short period of time if his or her diet and exercise habits are bad enough.

Obesity is a dangerous physical condition in its own right that also opens the door to other life-threatening illnesses. The various systems of obese individuals' bodies become disrupted due to the excess fat. As a result, they have an increased risk for high blood pressure, high cholesterol, heart disease, kidney and liver disease, breathing problems, sleep problems, early arthritis, diabetes, and depression.

The body must work extremely hard to metabolize the extra salt and sugar found in junk food, leading to fatigue and more serious health problems.

Salt and Hypertension

When the body takes in too much sodium from salty snacks, it needs to work harder to expel the excess that it does not need. Excess sodium throws the regulation of blood and cell fluids out of whack, as the body retains more water to compensate for the imbalance.

Prolonged excessive sodium consumption can also result in hypertension, or high blood pressure. This is a serious, even life-threatening, condition that causes the heart to pump the blood harder, resulting in damage to the cells lining the arteries. The veins, muscles, kidneys, and heart all must work harder. As a result, the risk of a heart attack increases.

Incredibly Disgusting Additives

When you pick out your favorite sugary or salty snack, read the food label. But don't think you're safe because the label says "natural ingredients" or "natural flavors." Upon closer examination, these ingredients can be quite unappetizing. Some items that are labeled "natural" can actually come from some quite shocking sources. Insect secretions, bone char, crushed red beetles, fertilizer such as ammonium sulfate, beaver anal glands, beef fat, lanolin (the oil from sheep's wool), duck feathers, coal tar, calf stomachs, and sand have all been used to "enhance" some of the foods we eat. These ingredients all fall under the category of "natural" additives.

Salt and Sugar: A Terrible Combination

The combination of high blood pressure caused by too much salt intake and insulin problems caused by too much sugar consumption makes the body constantly operate in overdrive. The body is running at top speed to metabolize sugars and expel excess sodium, even when it is at rest. Bones and joints also become strained from the extra weight gained as a result of a high sugar, high salt diet.

Rather than eating sugary and salty snacks only once in a rare while, children and adults alike are now suffering the ill effects of consuming these snacks, day after day, between their regular meals. And even their regular meals are often equally high in sugar and sodium. In recent years, doctors have observed an increase in kidney stones in young children. This is typically an illness associated with middle aged and elderly people. Yet one such patient was only eight months old! A kidney stone is a hard mass in the kidney, usually formed from calcium. Doctors feel the increase in such cases is due to salty foods. When too much salt is consumed, the body reacts by producing excess calcium in the urine. Many of the kidney stones now being found in children have high levels of calcium in them.

Broken bones among children have increased in recent years as well. Doctors feel this

This hard mass of calcium compounds is called a kidney stone. These stones are now being found in young children with too much salt in their diets.

is partially due to an alarming trend of replacing calcium-rich milk with arti-ficially sweetened fruit drinks and sodas. Calcium is a mineral that the body requires to help build strong teeth and bones.

Many common snack foods, such as potato chips, cookies, breakfast pas-tries, cream-filled snack cakes, cupcakes, donuts, pretzels, candy, ice cream, and gummy fruit snacks are all poor dietary choices. The excess sugars (arti-ficial or otherwise), salt or sodium, and artificial colors and flavors in these snacks are not what our bodies need to stay healthy. Consistently poor snack-ing habits will result in short-term ill effects. If not changed, however, they can lead to devastating long-term health issues that will result in a lifetime of obesity, disease, and even premature death.

3 —— LONG-TERM EFFECTS

A person may not think much about eating a candy bar with her lunch or salty potato chips as an after-school snack. She may not even be overweight at all. Even by the time she reaches her twenties, she may not become overweight or see any obvious negative effects from the sugary and salty snacks she eats regularly. Her body may have no problem metabolizing that mega-large tub of cake frosting or that giant bag of salty corn chips. But over a lifetime of eating snacks that clog arteries, constrict blood flow, and interfere with organ functions, her body will become as unhealthy and toxic as the unwholesome, incredibly disgusting snacks crowding the shelves in the grocery store, supermarket, and convenience store.

Obesity

Beyond the short-term effects of poor snacking habits, there are also devastating long-term effects of frequently indulging in incredibly disgusting foods. The body must work hard to carry the extra weight that one gains through unhealthy snacking. If one's diet is consistently poor, the workload on the body's systems becomes too much to handle. The long-term effects are devastating to the body's various systems and organs, and debilitating diseases result. The American Medical Association

This picture shows a cancerous bowel. Bowel cancer is one of the most common cancers in North America and is believed to be caused by poor eating habits.

believes that obesity plays an important role in the premature deaths of 280,000 U.S. citizens every year. According to the Research and Development Corporation and the University of Chicago, "More Americans are obese than smoke, use illegal drugs, or suffer from ailments unrelated to obesity."

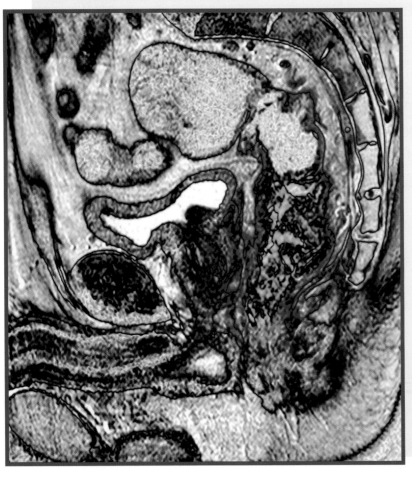

Friends Can Help

A recent study by the *New England Journal of Medicine* has shown that obesity can be contagious, in a sense, among friends. The thirty-two-year study showed that one's chances of becoming obese increased by 57 percent if a friend became obese. The inverse was also true—if a friend lost weight, one was more likely to do so as well. The conclusions drawn by the study's authors are that people are greatly influenced by their support network or community of family and friends and that more healthful eating habits—and inspiration to change—can spread throughout social networks.

An obese child runs the increased risk of carrying his or her poor eating habits into adulthood and remaining obese as an adult. This greatly increases his or her risk of cancer. The American Cancer Society has determined that obesity increases the risk for cancer of the breasts, ovaries, gall bladder, prostate, and colon.

Research now shows that childhood obesity may shorten a person's life span even if he or she does not remain obese as an adult. In women, childhood obesity can result in early menstruation, sometimes before age ten. Irregular or missed menstrual cycles can eventually result from obesity, too. Forty to 60 percent of women who contract cysts on their ovaries in adulthood are also obese.

Diabetes

Other devastating illnesses and complications arise from eating salty and sugary snacks. With the pancreas working harder than ever to produce enough

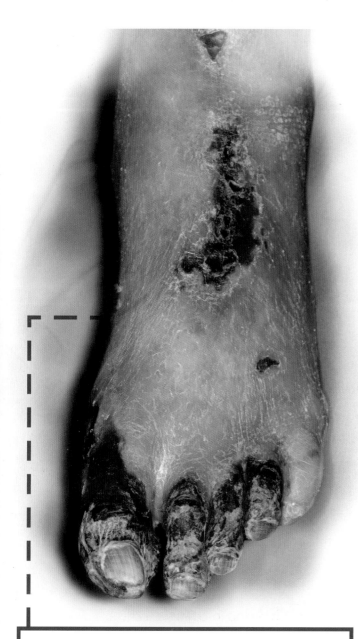

Diabetes can result in gangrene, which is the death of body tissues due to poor blood circulation.

insulin to regulate excessive levels of glucose (sugar) in the blood, a disease called diabetes can result. Over time, the body will become resistant to all the excess insulin being produced to control the high glucose levels. Once the body's cells become insulin resistant, blood sugar levels shoot up. Eventually, the pancreas wears out and cannot keep up. When this happens to a person and his or her body cannot produce or absorb enough insulin to regulate the glucose, diabetes has taken hold.

Diabetes is a health disorder that results when the body can no longer produce enough insulin on its own (type 1 diabetes) or the body's cells no longer respond to the insulin that is produced (also known as type 2 diabetes or insulin resistance). Type 1 diabetics are often born with the condition. It is often an inherited disease and therefore not related to poor diet. Type 2 diabetes, however, is more often developed over time as a result of dietary and lifestyle choices. Type 2 diabetes is common among those people who don't exercise, are overweight, smoke, and have a high-fat diet. Conversely, people who exercise regularly, have a healthy and low-fat diet, don't smoke, drink alcohol only in moderation, and maintain a normal weight reduce their chances of developing type 2 diabetes by almost 90 percent.

With type 2 or insulin-resistant diabetes, the body's cells no longer respond to insulin. They cannot absorb glucose well enough to obtain the energy they need to function properly. Unabsorbed by the cells, the glucose collects in the blood instead, and blood sugar rises to dangerous levels. Over time, the results can be very serious, gruesome, and even deadly. They include vision loss, nerve damage, amputation of limbs, cardiovascular disease, clogged arteries, heart attack, stroke, kidney and liver disease and failure, coma, and even death.

New and disturbing medical terms have emerged due to the overconsumption of unhealthy sugary and salty snack foods. "Prehypertension" and "prediabetes" are new terms being used to describe high blood pressure and type 2 diabetes in children and young adults. In previous generations, hypertension and type 2 diabetes were associated with late middle age or elderly people. They were very rare in children, teenagers, and even young adults. Previously, the diabetes most commonly found in children was the inherited type 1 diabetes. Type 2 diabetes even used to be called adult onset diabetes, while type 1 was known as juvenile diabetes. But more and more

Deposits of fat in the arteries cause clogs that make it difficult for blood to flow properly. This can be a deadly effect of poor eating habits, resulting in heart attacks or strokes.

children are now developing type 2 diabetes, the type of diabetes usually found in adults and caused by dietary and lifestyle choices. The medical community is being forced to rename these diseases because the unhealthy North American diet is causing younger and younger people to develop illnesses that once struck far later in life.

Cardiovascular Disease

Increased sodium levels in the body can raise a person's blood pressure, as can increased glucose levels. Poor snack choices—salty and sugary junk food— result in elevated sodium and glucose levels. High blood pressure is caused by an imbalance of fluid regulation due to excess sodium intake. According to the American Heart Association, there are almost seventy-five million people in the United States age twenty and older who have high blood pressure. This represents one in three adults.

Reducing sodium intake to acceptable levels will help lower blood pressure and put less stress on the heart, arteries, and kidneys. When there is too much stress on these parts of the body, a person can suffer a heart attack, kidney failure, or a stroke. People with high blood pressure often need to take medication for the rest of their lives in order to keep their blood pressure under control, and their life expectancy is shorter than average. Weight loss is a key ingredient to lowering blood pressure and reversing its harmful effects.

Diet, Disease, and Quality of Life

Extensive studies have linked cancer, diabetes, heart disease, and stroke to a lifetime of poor diet. These diseases are less common in parts of the world where diets are healthier than ours and people consume far fewer sugary and salty snacks. Living with these life-threatening ailments can make a person's life unbearable and rob him or her of valuable years of healthy living with family and friends. Spending many hours at the doctor's office, getting tests, being unable to work and make money, and missing out on travel, adventures, and other fun outings with friends and family is no way to live.

So before you reach for that incredibly salty chicken finger or incredibly sugary toaster pastry, remember that many of these long-term, diet-related ailments are not easily reversible or even curable. Chances are they will kill you, but only after making your life utterly miserable first.

MYTHS AND FACTS

Myth: Snacks low in fat will not make us fat.
Fact: Sugar has no fat content at all, but our bodies convert the sugar directly into fat.

Myth: Adding sugar or salt to homemade food is a bad idea.
Fact: Cooking for yourself and sweetening and salting your food moderately will likely result in less sugary and salty meals than those found in the frozen or prepared food aisle or at fast-food and other kinds of restaurants. Processed and prepared (not homemade) foods are usually very high in sodium, salt, and/or artificial sweeteners.

Myth: People who are overweight as children will be unhealthy for the rest of their lives.
Fact: It is always possible for people to change their eating habits and improve their health at any age.

4 — EAT HEALTHY SNACKS NOW!

Remember that sugary and salty snack foods like ice cream, crackers, salted nuts, fruit chews, chocolate, cheese puffs, and puddings are perfectly fine to eat in small quantities and on special occasions. The problem is that the "special occasion" has become several times a day for many people. Some people even eat snacks in place of real, wholesome, well-balanced meals and have little knowledge of how to snack healthfully.

When someone consumes too many pretzels, energy bars, potato chips, and cookies, he gets filled up and loses his taste for fruits, vegetables, and whole grains. He is then less likely to eat healthy foods that can be beneficial to his body. These healthier, unprocessed, "whole food" snacking alternatives contain natural sugars and salt. These natural sugars and salt are found in lower levels than the large amount of salt and sugar or sugar substitutes found in processed snack food. Yet with so many packaged snacks conveniently

Baking your own snacks helps you to control the amount of sugar and salt you are consuming.

located for sale in schools, malls, stores, and rest stops—and so few healthy alternatives for sale beside them—it becomes hard to make the right choice.

Many times there are simply no healthy choices at all, and this can be very frustrating and discouraging. Yet some simple steps can be taken to ensure healthier snacking, and new habits can be started immediately. Remember the time to change is right now. Breaking old bad habits in favor of new good ones that involve more healthy choices can help you snack right for the rest of your life.

How to Snack Well and Stay Healthy

One way to snack healthfully is to make your own snacks. Snacks such as banana breads, cakes, cookies, puddings, dried fruit, pretzels, and popcorn that are overly sugary or salty when bought in a store can all be made more healthfully in the home. They can be prepared simply and from a few basic ingredients. Making these foods from scratch allows you to control the amount of sugar and salt that go into them. There are also far fewer ingredients—such as preservatives, thickeners, and artificial sweeteners and colors—in homemade treats than in the processed, packaged versions.

Making homemade snack foods takes time, and it may not be something you can do every day. The upside of this, however, is that these homemade snack treats will be eaten less frequently and on more special occasions. To keep snacks like these fresh and prevent overeating, make them in advance and freeze or refrigerate them at home. Take one or two of them with you before you leave the house in the morning. A couple of cookies as a treat is something that can be eaten between meals only once in a while, not daily.

The Importance of Reading Nutrition Labels

When choosing from store-bought snacks, one needs to become a detective of sorts to sift through the ingredients and nutrition labels, seeking out serving size, added sugars, and sodium content. The serving size will let you know, for example, that if you have a huge bag of corn chips in front of you, only eleven chips represents one complete serving. If you sit down and eat the entire bag, you've consumed about 10 servings, over 1,200 calories (about half your daily requirement). These ten servings eaten all at once have provided more than 50 percent of your daily sodium intake and 100 percent of your daily fat intake.

Packaged foods provide nutrition labels to help consumers track their consumption of various nutrients. Sugar and salt amounts are usually listed in grams and milligrams.

- - How to Read a Food Label - - -

All packaged foods in the United States must have a food label called Nutri-tion Facts. Checking the label is an important part of eating healthy for a lifetime. First check the serving size. Sometimes a serving size is less than half of what a packaged snack contains. This means that a sealed package containing two toaster pastries may in fact be two servings, not one. So the per serving calorie count you find on the label is for only one of those pastries, not both. Next check the sodium and sugar content. Remember that we should eat no more than 1.4 ounces (40 g) of sugar and 0.08 ounces (2,400 mg) of sodium in a single day. All of the foods' ingredients are listed according to weight, from highest to lowest. Sometimes several different kinds of sweeteners will be listed in an attempt to keep sugar off the top of the list. If you see two or three sweeteners listed just below the first ingredient, chances are there is more sugar in the snack than anything else.

It is important to look for this information on a food label. By finding it, you will learn that your big bag of chips is not an individual snack size and should be shared with as many as a dozen people. If you are alone, make sure to place the suggested serving size in a cup or on a plate. Do not eat from the bag, box, or snack food package, and do not go back for seconds.

Calorie content is another thing to look for on snack food labels. On average, men and women require only around 1,700 to 2,200 calories a day. Recommended total daily calories varies depending on a person's height, weight, age, and activity level. A distance runner would require more calo-ries throughout the day because she is burning more calories. Someone

Fresh foods such as carrots are a healthy way to snack without adding extra sugar or salt to your body.

who doesn't exercise and isn't very physically active throughout the day requires far fewer calories. That person's body is using less energy than a runner's does, so it requires less input of food energy.

Get Your Daily Servings of Fruits, Vegetables, and Exercise!

It is important to stay physically active by getting about an hour of exercise a day. It is also vital to design a healthy diet that will keep the body in shape and keep one's heart and metabolism working efficiently. A small snack should be limited to 100–200 calories. Carefully monitor added sweeteners and sodium in these snacks to make sure you are not getting too much sugar or salt for the day.

Above all else, the healthiest foods to snack on are fruits, nuts, vegetables, and whole grains. Celery and carrots are great portable snacks. Coupled with some homemade salsa or ranch dressing, or served plain, these are tasty treats to eat between meals or when you are on the go. Nuts such as cashews, walnuts, peanuts, and almonds are all very healthy snack foods when eaten in moderation. Remember to buy unsalted nuts whenever possible or you may be getting too much sodium in one sitting. Some nuts, such as pistachios, come heavily salted and should be avoided except in small quantities. Some nuts also come honey-roasted with a coating of added sweetener on them. These, too, are less healthy and should be snacked on in moderation. Raw, unroasted nuts are the best choice.

Making healthy food choices takes practice. And don't forget that you can have your favorite salty and sugary snacks once in a while. Just remember that the rest of the time you should be making an effort to avoid incredibly dis-gusting snacks. You can do it, and there are a lot of reasons to change for the better now. By switching to healthier, more natural snacks, you may be saving your own life!

TEN GREAT QUESTIONS TO ASK A NUTRITIONIST

1: How can I avoid unhealthy foods when I am out with friends at the movies, the mall, a restaurant, or a sports event?

2: How can I lose weight if I am overweight?

3: What can I do if I am at someone's house and they serve sugary or salty snacks?

4: How would I know if I have diabetes or high blood pressure?

5: Should I avoid all foods that have high fructose corn syrup or other ingredients that take the place of sugar?

6: Am I healthy if I am a normal weight?

7: Can I eat whatever I want if I'm not overweight?

8: How can I make a decision about foods that do not have a nutrition label, such as fresh or prepared foods from a bakery, deli, or restaurant?

9: How can I help to get healthier snack choices in my school vending machines?

10: What is organic sugar and salt? Is organic sugar or salt healthier than regular sugar or salt?

GLOSSARY

body mass index Weight-to-height ratio used to determine if someone is overweight; also known as BMI.

calorie A unit of heat energy that humans and other animals get from food.

cancer A disease caused by abnormal cell division in a certain part of the body.

diabetes A disease in which the pancreas does not produce enough insulin or the body's cells become resistant to the insulin the pancreas produces. This results in poor glucose absorption by the cells and high blood sugar levels.

glucose A simple sugar that is needed for energy in living things.

high fructose corn syrup A corn-based artificial sweetener placed in processed foods as a sugar substitute.

hypertension High blood pressure, a condition caused by increased pressure of the blood in the arteries.

insulin A hormone made by the pancreas that regulates how much glucose is in the blood.

obese Above a body weight considered normal, with a BMI above 30.

overweight Above a body weight considered normal, with a BMI of 25 to 30.

pancreas A gland in the body that aids in digestion by producing insulin.

sodium A chemical element needed by the body to regulate fluids.

stroke A sudden attack caused by an interruption of the blood flow to the brain.

FOR MORE INFORMATION

Centers for Disease Control and Prevention (CDC)

1600 Clifton Road

Atlanta, GA 30333

(800) CDC-INFO (232-4636)

Web site: http://www.cdc.gov

The CDC's mission is to collaborate to create the expertise, information, and tools that people and communities need to protect their health—through health promotion; prevention of disease, injury, and disability; and preparedness for new health threats.

Children's Health Foundation

400 West Main Street, Suite 210

Aspen, CO 81611

(888) 920-4750

Web site: http://www.childrenshealthfoundation.net

The Children's Health Foundation is a nonprofit organization dedicated to making changes in schools and communities that promote health, including the prevention of childhood obesity.

Diabetic Children's Foundation

785 Plymouth, Suite 210

Mont Royal, QC H4P 1B3

Canada

(800) 731-9683

Web site: http://diabetes-children.ca

The Diabetic Children's Foundation promotes the health of Canadian children and teens who are living with diabetes. The foundation also has a summer camp for its members.

Health Canada

Address Locator 0900C2

Ottawa, ON KIA 0K9

Canada

(866) 225-0709

Web site: http://www.hc-sc.gc.ca/index-eng.php

Health Canada is the federal department responsible for helping Canadians maintain and improve their health.

International Food Information Council Foundation

1100 Connecticut Avenue NW, Suite 430

Washington, DC 20036

(202) 296-6540

Web site: http://www.foodinsight.org

The International Food Information Council Foundation is an independent, nonprofit organization dedicated to public education about food, nutrition, and food safety.

National Institutes of Health (NIH)

9000 Rockville Pike

Bethesda, MD 20892

(301) 496-4000

Web site: http://www.nih.gov/index.html

NIH's mission is to seek fundamental knowledge about the nature and behavior of living systems and the application of that knowledge to enhance health, lengthen life, and reduce the burdens of illness and disability.

School Nutrition Association

120 Waterfront Street, Suite 300

National Harbor, MD 20745

(301) 686-3100

Web site: http://www.schoolnutrition.org

The School Nutrition Association provides education and training to those interested in advancing the nutrition of school lunches and providing nutritious meals to children.

Shaping America's Youth

120 NW 9th Avenue, Suite 216

Portland, OR 97209-3326

(800) SAY-9221 (729-9221)

Web site: http://www.shapingamericasyouth.org

Shaping America's Youth is a group that provides information about community programs across the United States that attempt to increase physical activity and improve nutrition among American children.

Web Sites

Due to the changing nature of Internet links, Rosen Publishing has developed an online list of Web sites related to the subject of this book. This site is updated regularly. Please use this link to access this list:

http://www.rosenlinks.com/idf/snac

FOR FURTHER READING

Carle, Megan, and Jill Carle. *Teens Cook: How to Cook What You Want to Eat.* New York, NY: Ten Speed Press, 2004.

Gold, Rozanne. *Eat Fresh Food: Awesome Recipes for Teen Chefs.* New York, NY: Bloomsbury USA, 2009.

Grunes, Barbara. *Diabetes Snacks, Treats, & Easy Eats for Kids: 130 Recipes for the Foods Kids Really Like to Eat.* Chicago, IL: Surrey Books, 2006.

Platt, Richard. *They Ate What?! The Weird History of Food.* Minneapolis, MN: T&N Children's Publishing, 2006.

Pollan, Michael. *The Omnivore's Dilemma for Kids: The Secrets Behind What You Eat* (Young Readers Edition). New York, NY: Dial, 2009.

Schlosser, Eric, and Charles Wilson. *Chew on This: Everything You Don't Want to Know About Fast Food.* New York, NY: Sandpiper, 2007.

Schuh, Mari C., and Barbara J. Rolls. *Healthy Snacks.* Mankato, MN: Coughlan Publishing, 2006.

Spurlock, Morgan. *Don't Eat This Book: Fast Food and the Supersizing of America.* New York, NY: Berkeley Trade, 2006.

Stern, Sam, and Susan Stern. *Cooking Up a Storm: The Teen Survival Cookbook.* New York, NY: Candlewick Press, 2006.

Stern, Sam, and Susan Stern. *Get Cooking.* New York, NY: Candlewick Press, 2009.

Zinczenko, David, and Matt Goulding. *Eat This, Not That!* New York, NY: Rodale Press, 2008.

BIBLIOGRAPHY

Bakalar, Nicholas. "Fructose-Sweetened Beverages Linked to Heart Risks."
New York Times, April 23, 2009. Retrieved December 2009 (http://
www.nytimes.com/2009/04/23/health/23sugar.html?scp=1&sq=Fructose-
Sweetened%20Beverages%20Linked%20to%20Heart%20
Risks&st=cse).

Critser, Greg. *Fat Land: How Americans Became the Fattest People in the World.*
New York, NY: Houghton Mifflin Company, 2003.

Hodgen, Donald A. "Global Snack Food Industry Trends." AllBusiness.com,
July 1, 2004. Retrieved December 2009 (http://www.allbusiness.com/
retail-trade/food-beverage-stores-specialty-food/202589-1.html).

Iasevoli, Brenda. "A Plan to Cut Sugar in Schools." *Time for Kids*, February 10,
2004. Retrieved December 2009 (http://www.timeforkids.com/TFK/kids/
news/story/0,28277,585047,00.html).

Kolata, Gina. "Study Says Obesity Can Be Contagious." *New York Times*,
July 25, 2007. Retrieved February 2010 (http://www.nytimes.com/2007/
07/25/health/25cnd-fat.html).

Medina, Jennifer. "In Schools, New Rules on Snacks for Sale." *New York Times*,
October 6, 2009. Retrieved December 2009 (http://www.nytimes.com/
2009/10/07/nyregion/07contract.html).

Okie, Susan. *Fed Up! Winning the War Against Childhood Obesity.* Washington,
DC: Joseph Henry Press, 2005.

Poirot, Carolyn. "High-Fructose Corn Syrup Fueling Obesity Epidemic, Doctors
Say." *Seattle Times*, December 4, 2005. Retrieved December 2009 (http://
seattletimes.nwsource.com/html/health/2002658491_healthsyrup04.html).

Pollan, Michael. *In Defense of Food.* New York, NY: Penguin, 2008.

Pollan, Michael. *The Omnivore's Dilemma: A Natural History of Four Meals.* New York, NY: Penguin, 2006.

PR Newswire. "Kids Breaking More Bones: Doctors Say Soft Drinks Poor Substitute for Milk." TheFreeLibrary.com, March 23, 2004. Retrieved December 2009 (http://www.thefreelibrary.com/Kids+Breaking+More+Bones%3B+-+Doctors+Say+Soft+Drinks+Poor+Substitute...-a0114523014).

RSC.org. "Why Do We Need Salt?" Retrieved December 2009 (http://www.rsc.org/Chemsoc/Chembytes/HotTopics/Salt/whysalt.asp).

Schlosser, Eric. *Fast Food Nation.* New York, NY: Harper Perennial, 2002.

Tanner, Lindsey. "Doctors Say Kidney Stones in Kids on the Rise." Physorg.com, March 26, 2009. Retrieved December 2009 (http://www.physorg.com/news157300490.html).

Tartamella, Lisa, Elaine Herscher, and Chris Woolston. *Generation Extra Large: Rescuing Our Children from the Epidemic of Obesity.* New York, NY: Basic Books, 2006.

Zinczenko, David, and Matt Goulding. *Eat This, Not That!* New York, NY: Rodale Press, 2010.

INDEX

A

American Cancer Society, 25
American Heart Association, 13, 24, 28
arthritis, 18

B

body mass index, 12

C

cancer, 25, 29
Centers for Disease Control and
    Prevention, 15

D

Department of Education, 15
depression, 18
diabetes, 8, 13, 18, 25–28, 29, 39

E

electrolytes, 12, 13

F

Food and Drug Administration, 9, 12
food labels, 6, 8, 11, 20, 34–37

G

glucose, 9, 17, 26, 27, 28

H

healthy snacks, eating, 31–38
heart disease, 12, 18, 27, 28–29
high blood pressure/hypertension, 12, 13,
    18, 19, 20, 27, 28–29, 39
high fructose corn syrup, 7–8, 9, 39

I

insulin, 17, 20, 26–27

K

kidney stones, 12, 21

N

New England Journal of Medicine, 25
nutritionist, questions to ask a, 39

O

obesity, 8, 9, 12, 13, 15, 18, 22, 23–25
osteoporosis, 12

About the Author

Adam Furgang is a writer who has written several books on science, health, and nutrition topics, including *Carbonated Beverages: The Incredibly Disgusting Story*. He lives in upstate New York with his wife and two children.

Photo Credits

Cover (top), pp. 1, 4–5 © www.istockphoto.com/Sharon Dominick; cover (middle), pp. 6, 16, 23, 31 (middle) Tom Grill/Iconica/Getty Images; cover (bottom), pp. 6, 16, 23, 31 (bottom) © www.istockphoto.com/Shane White; p. 7 UpperCut Images/Getty Images; p. 9 Susanna Price/Dorling Kindersley/Getty Images; p. 11 © www.istockphoto.com/steve vanhorn; pp. 14–15 Paul J. Richards/AFP/Getty Images; p. 18 Stephan Gladieu/Getty Images; p. 19 Hemera/Thinkstock; p. 21 Hank Morgan—Rainbow/Science Faction/Getty Images; p. 24 © Science Photo Library/Custom Medical Stock Photo; p. 26 © Scott Camazine/Photo Researchers, Inc.; pp. 28–29 © www.istockphoto.com/jamesbenet; p. 32 Comstock/Thinkstock; p. 34 © www.istockphoto.com/Sean Locke; pp. 36–37 Jenny Acheson/Riser/Getty Images.

Designer: Les Kanturek; Photo Researcher: Amy Feinberg